A WINNING SKILLS BOOK

You Can Have a Great Future!

Joy Berry

Illustrated by Bartholomew

Joy Berry
Enterprises

Copyright © Joy Berry, 2022
Originally Published 2013

All rights are reserved.

No part of this book can be duplicated or used without the prior written permission of the copyright owner, except for the use of brief quotations from the book.

For inquiries or permission requests contact the publisher.

Published by Joy Berry Enterprises
www.joyberryenterprises.com

Joy Berry
Enterprises

You can have a great future if you understand
- three basic human activities,
- work,
- play,
- regeneration,
- the importance of living a well-balanced life,
- how to start living a well-balanced life,
- how to develop a well-balanced life for the future, and
- six wise saying about a successful future.

THREE BASIC HUMAN ACTIVITIES

Most people's lives consist of three basic activities.

These three basic activities are:
- work,
- play, and
- regeneration.

Work is survival activity. It is what people do to sustain their lives.

Work includes the activities people do to
- take care of themselves,
- maintain healthy relationships with others, and
- take care of the environment in which they live.

WORK

Almost all work has some elements that are difficult or unpleasant to do. Therefore, work often requires energy and effort that people are not naturally inclined to give.

Although work can be difficult or unpleasant, it can produce worthwhile results. However most of the benefits derived from work are not experienced immediately. Instead they are experienced after the work has been completed. This is called **delayed gratification**.

In addition to whatever results work produces, some of the delayed gratification received from work is the fulfillment of a person's normal need to
- be responsible,
- be constructive (achieve worthwhile things), and
- contribute something to the world in which he or she lives.

Some of the delayed gratification received from work includes feelings of
- worth,
- accomplishment, and
- fulfillment.

Play is pleasurable activity. It is what people do to make their lives enjoyable.

Play includes the activities people do to
- temporarily escape from reality,
- have fun, and
- feel good.

Almost all play is pleasant and something people want to do. Therefore, it requires no more energy or effort than a person is naturally motivated to give.

Most of the benefits derived from play are experienced right away, while the activity is in progress. This is called **immediate gratification**.

Some of the immediate gratification received from play is the fulfillment of a person's normal need to
- be distracted from the stress and strains of everyday life,
- release tension, and
- express pent-up emotions.

Some of the immediate gratification received from play is the fulfillment of a person's normal need to
- smile and laugh,
- be frivolous, and
- feel joyful.

Regeneration is replenishing activity. It is what people do to rejuvenate themselves.

Regeneration includes activities that people do to rejuvenate themselves
- physically,
- mentally,
- emotionally, and
- spiritually.

REJUVENATION

Some rejuvenation activities replenish something that has been expended, such as physical energy. Other rejuvenation activities fulfill various personal quests, such as some people's quest to know God.

Because rejuvenation activities often replace something that is missing, normal people are usually naturally motivated to do them. Eating, relaxation, sleep, conversations that deal with personal issues, and meditation are examples of rejuvenation activities.

THE IMPORTANCE OF LIVING A WELL-BALANCED LIFE

There are two basic kinds of adults: those who are healthy, happy, and successful and those who are not.

Healthy, happy, successful adults live **balanced** lives that include reasonable amounts of work, play, and rejuvenation activities.

THE IMPORTANCE OF LIVING A WELL-BALANCED LIFE

Adults who are not healthy, happy, or successful live **unbalanced** lives in which they do only one or two types of activities, while they neglect the others.

Most well-balanced adults spend an approximate daily average of
- 8 hours working,
- 4 hours playing, and
- 12 hours rejuvenating themselves.

An exception to this is adults who, by working more intensely and/or more efficiently, are able to accomplish more per hour and, therefore, are able to work less.

Another exception is adults who derive so much pleasure from their work they do not require much time for play.

THE IMPORTANCE OF LIVING A WELL-BALANCED LIFE

Well-balanced adults get the maximum benefits from every activity. They do not allow themselves to be distracted. They focus their complete attention on what they are doing. They concentrate on work when they are working and do not think about anything else. They do the same thing with play and regeneration.

Well-balanced adults also give their very best effort to whatever they are doing so they can produce the best possible results.

THE IMPORTANCE OF LIVING A WELL-BALANCED LIFE

If you want to become healthy, happy, and successful, you need to work toward becoming an adult who lives a well-balanced life.

The first step to doing this is to start becoming a person who lives a well-balanced life.

Here are two reasons for beginning at an early age to live a well-balanced life.
- Living a well-balanced life is not something a person does automatically when he or she becomes and adult. It is a lifestyle that has to be carefully developed and then practiced if it is to be perfected.
- A balanced life works only if it is habitual, since people who have to talk themselves into it everyday seldom follow through on a consistent basis.

30 HOW TO START LIVING A WELL-BALANCED LIFE

You can determine whether you are living a balanced life by doing the following:

During a specific seven-day period (preferably Monday through Sunday), keep track of the amount of time you spend doing each type of activity in a 24-hour period.

At the end of the seven-day period, add up all the hours you spent working (school and homework are work). Add up the hours you spent playing. Then add up the hours you spent regenerating.
- The hours you spend working should be close to 56.
- The hours you spend playing should be close to 28.
- The hours you spend rejuvenating should be close to 84.

If you find that your numbers are much higher or lower than the normal averages, you need to re-evaluate what you are doing. You might decide that you need to spend more time doing one activity and less time doing another.

Here's another way to determine whether your life is out of balance.

Pay attention to recurring emotions such as
- boredom,
- frustration,
- anxiety,
- guilt,
- feelings of futility, or
- a sense of worthlessness.

Recurring emotions that cause you to feel uncomfortable might be an indication that your life is out of balance. If this is the case, the only way to rid yourself of the uncomfortable feelings is to put your life in balance.

HOW TO DEVELOP A WELL-BALANCED LIFE FOR THE FUTURE

Once your current life is in balance, you can begin to make plans for your adult life (your life after you turn 18 years of age), This requires four basic steps.

Step 1: Establish future goals.

Decide exactly how, as an adult you would like to spend your time
- working,
- playing, and
- regenerating.

It is important to be realistic about your goals. Choose ones that
- you are actually capable of doing and
- you genuinely want to achieve.

Get help from relatives, friends, or professionals (such as school or career counselors) if you have difficulty formulating realistic goals.

36 HOW TO DEVELOP A WELL-BALANCED LIFE FOR THE FUTURE

Step 2: Sort your goals.

Sort your goal into 5-year increments. Determine what you would like to do for the first five years after the age of 18, the second five years, and so on.

> LET'S SEE...IF I'M GOING TO BE A PERFORMER, I'LL NEED SOME TRAINING. I'LL ALSO NEED TO SUPPORT MYSELF WHILE I'M WAITING FOR MY BIG BREAK. SO, FOR THE FIRST FIVE YEARS I'LL GO TO A SCHOOL WHERE I CAN MAJOR IN PERFORMING ARTS AND GET MY TEACHING CREDENTIAL, I CAN WORK AS A LIVE-IN NANNY TO PAY FOR MY TUITION AND...

Don't worry if you have several careers you would like to pursue. Most healthy adults have from three to five careers during their lifetime.

Also, don't worry if you are unable to plan past the first or second five years, because it is the first five years that are most important for you to consider when you are young.

Step 3: List what needs to be done.

Write down exactly what needs to be done to prepare yourself for the first five years of your adult life. List tasks in the order that they need to be accomplished.

One way to get the information you need is to talk to or study the lives of adults who are doing anything similar to what you would like to do. Find out what they did to get where they got and what they recommend to people who would like to follow in their footsteps.

Another thing you can do is to get information and recommendations from professional organizations that represent the professions you want to pursue. Consult your local library for specific names, addresses, and telephone numbers.

Also, ask your school counselor or a professional career counselor for information.

Step 4: Do you need to do. Follow through with the things you need to do to achieve your goals.

A good future does not "just happen." You have to **work** to create a good future for yourself.

Generally speaking, the more preparation you put into your future, the greater the chances that it will turn out the way you want.

Conversely, the less you prepare for your future, the less it is likely to turn out the way you want.

It is important to always have a **fallback position** for every goal.

More often than not, initial plans have to be modified or scrapped altogether. When this happens, it is a good idea to be prepared with a back-up plan. A back-up plan is one that can replace a plan that has failed.

You always need a back-up plan in case your original plan does not work out.

There are six wise saying that can provide significant insights about creating a great future.

Wise Saying #1: You are your own bottom line.

You are responsible for your own life. No one else can live it for you. Therefore, it is important that you avoid planning a future in which another person takes care of you or is responsible for your success.

It is important for you to become an independent person who can function successfully on your own.

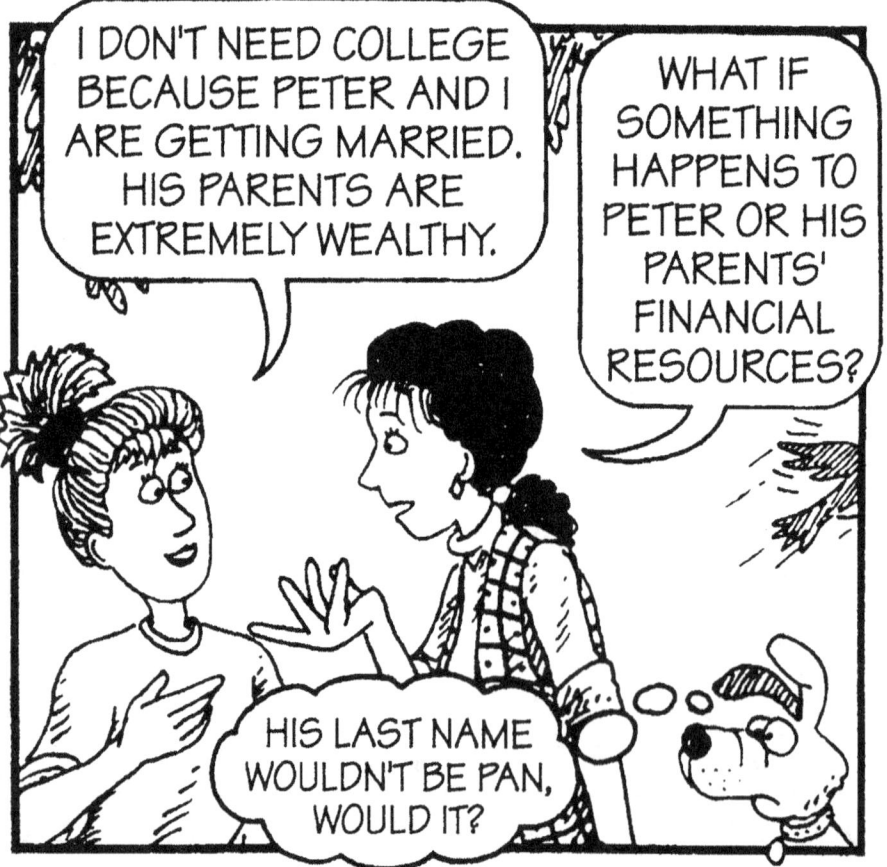

SIX SAYINGS ABOUT A SUCCESSFUL FUTURE 43

Wise Saying #2: No guts, no glory.

If you want the glory that comes from success, you have to be bold about pursuing it. You have to venture out and try doing the things that will bring you success, even if there is a chance you might fail. You must be willing to exchange a comfortable, predictable life for one in which you are willing to gamble on the hope that things could be much better if you did certain things to make them better.

SIX SAYINGS ABOUT A SUCCESSFUL FUTURE

Wise Saying #3: No pain, no gain.

There is always some discomfort associated with doing the tasks that must be done in order to progress. If you are not willing to endure this discomfort, you will not make any progress. This means that in order to succeed, it might be necessary for you to do things that you do not particularly enjoy or *want* to do.

Wise Saying #4: Anything worth having is worth working for.

Nothing in life is free. Everything must be earned. It takes work to earn anything. The only way to acquire something of value is to work for it. Therefore, if you are not willing to work for something you claim you want, it is doubtful that you genuinely want it.

Wise Saying #5: You get out of life what you put into it.

If you do nothing, you will achieve nothing, because the only way to achieve something is to do something. Therefore, the more you do, the more you will achieve, and the more you achieve, the greater your chances of being truly successful.

Wise Saying #6: The greater the effort, the greater the reward.

The amount of success you achieve will most likely be proportionate to the amount of work you put into it. Therefore, the more you work to attain success, the more successful you will most likely become.

48 CONCLUSION

With some careful planning and hard work, you can develop and live a well-balanced life. And this is the key to your having a great future.

www.ingramcontent.com/pod-product-compliance
Lightning Source LLC
Chambersburg PA
CBHW081409070526
44583CB00020B/2736